America's ★ ★ ★ Birthday

by Vita Richman

Scott Foresman
is an imprint of

Glenview, Illinois • Boston, Massachusetts • Chandler, Arizona
Upper Saddle River, New Jersey

ISBN 13: 978-0-328-51333-8
ISBN 10:   0-328-51333-4

17 16

What do you imagine when you think about the Fourth of July? Is it the flags waving in the wind? Is it the parade? Or the marching bands? Is it the family barbecue and the fireworks?

The Fourth of July is a great holiday in the United States. It is a birthday party for our country. It is on the day America decided to be free from England. This happened more than two hundred years ago, on July 4, 1776.

The first celebration of the Fourth of July took place in Massachusetts in 1781. Now you can see celebrations all over our country. Bands play. Fireworks light up the sky.

The flag is an important symbol of our country. A symbol is an image used to remind you of something. The flag reminds us of the United States. One of its nicknames is the Stars and Stripes.

Another symbol of our country is Uncle Sam. He wears a top hat, a vest, and a long jacket. He has stars on his hat. His trousers are striped. Sometimes people dress up like Uncle Sam in parades.

This man is dressed as Uncle Sam. People also draw Uncle Sam as a cartoon.

The Liberty Bell is a symbol of freedom. It is in Philadelphia at Independence Hall. The Liberty Bell was made in 1752. It cracked when it was rung for the first time! This bell had to be remade two more times. The last bell was rung for the final time in 1846. It cracked too much to fix.

Liberty Bell

Parades are a big part of the Fourth of July holiday. Marching bands, baton twirlers, baseball teams, and fire trucks may all take part in the parade. Many people cheer at the parade. They also wave U.S. flags.

A Fourth of July parade in Pittsfield, Massachusetts, USA

After a parade, many people have a picnic. Some people have a barbecue in a park or on the beach. Fireworks light up the sky in many towns. The fireworks can be the same colors as the flag: red, white, and blue.

Families eat holiday foods at the park.

Freedom is important for many countries around the world. People in India celebrate their country's freedom on August 15. Mexicans celebrate freedom on September 16.

For people in the United States, the Fourth of July is a very important date. Many people worked very hard for America to be free. The next time you see a Fourth of July parade, remember what it is all about!